Elf Village
Coloring Book

An Adult Coloring Book Featuring Adorable and Whimsical Elves Full of Holiday Fun and Christmas Cheer

Copyright 2019 © Coloring Book Cafe
All Rights Reserved.

Copyright @ 2019 Coloring Book Cafe
All Rights Reserved.

All rights reserved. No part of this publication may be reproduced or used in any form or by any means-- graphic, electronic, or mechanical, including photocopying, recording, or information storage-and-retrieval-- without permission of the publisher.

The designs in this book are intended for the personal, noncommercial use of the retail purchaser and are under federal copyright laws; they are not to be reproduced in any form for commercial use. Permission is granted to photocopy content for the personal use of the retail purchaser.

an Imprint of **The Fruitful Mind Publishing LTD.**
www.coloringbookcafe.com

Have questions? Let us know.
support@coloringbookcafe.com

BONUS

Relax And Create Your Own Masterpiece With
THIS 30 PAGE FREE *Beautiful Adult Coloring Book*

Claim Your FREE Coloring Book at:

www.freecoloringbooklet.com

Made in the USA
San Bernardino, CA
11 February 2020